What I Think When I Think Of Love

Samruddhi Jadhav

BookLeaf Publishing

India | USA | UK

Presentation by *BookLeaf Publishing*

Web: www.bookleafpub.com

E-mail: info@bookleafpub.com

ISBN: 9789363317802

First edition 2024

To all the beating hearts out there,

'I wish the person you love and the person you make love to are the same.'

-sunkissed

When They First Met

she was
a rainbow girl,
full of colors
and
he was
the monochrome boy,
swaying between
black and white

it was
nothing less than magic
when they met
and
the world was in awe,

because,
her colors never seemed
so brighter,
if it wasn't for him
and
his monochromatic dilemma
never made more sense
if it wasn't for her

He Is The Sun

he is the sun,
rising in her
barren heart

and
illuminating
the darkest voids
residing there

Golden Kiss

every morning
the sun rises
in my soul

as you
kiss me golden
at dawn
in our vivid
world of dreams

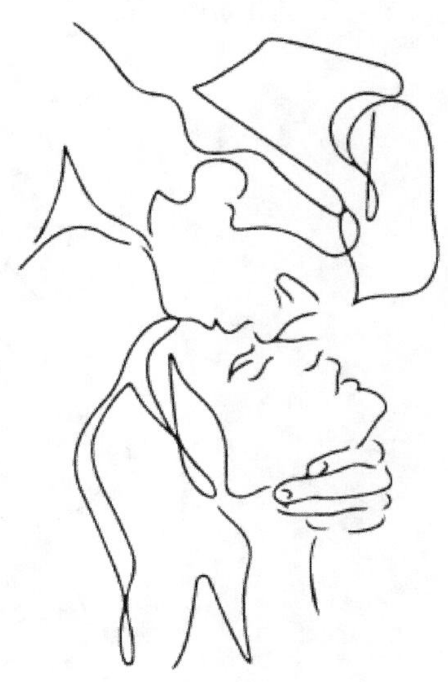

I Wonder

sometimes
i wonder,

when you look at me
with your
big fervent eyes,

like
i am the only one
you wish to look at
for the rest of your life

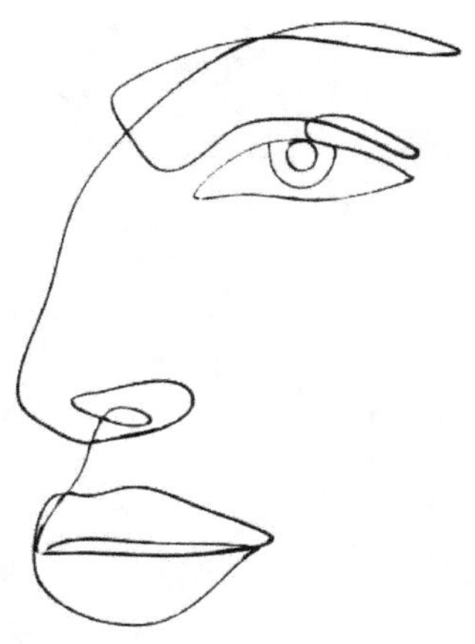

The Reason

i am always me,

you are always you,

but i am more myself
when i am with you

and you are more yourself
when you are with me

isn't this the reason why
i like you
and
you like me?

Love Is An Art

your fingers caress
my ecstatic face
like brushstrokes
on the canvas

and
like a gifted artist,
you fill
not just colors
but the soul
in my desolate body

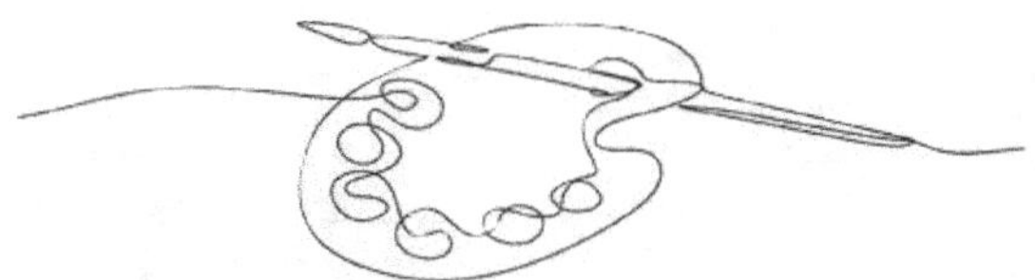

You Calm Me

you whisper
in my ears
how splendid i am
and
not just beautiful

your touch
builds unquenchable fire
in me

and
as we burn,
it calms
the snowstorm of love
inside me

Besotted

since i first met you,
my eyes couldn't see
anything else,
not when you're around
but also,
when you're just a mirage
from my memories

i wonder,
how someone could be
so besotted
by the existence
of someone,
that it makes
everything else
simply irrelevant
and gets
almost possessed
with this very
thought of love

just like
i am besotted
with you right now

and
i want you
to make my art flourish
by being my forever muse,
but even if you choose
to be nothing
but just
my momentary musing,
the artist in me
would still admire you
the way you've
never been admired

A Lazy Afternoon With You

on a lazy afternoon like this,
i try to focus on this novel undone
but then i look at you
sleeping next to me

your face looks like a baby
with that lazy drool
on your chubby flush cheeks
and your arms folded
in a funny formal way
for some unexplainable reason

it makes my lips go concave
to think that i love this silly man
and i run my fingers through
your messy but soft hair
i know you love it when
i pamper you like this
maybe that's why
i don't do it more often
until you ask for it
just to tease you

oh,
i don't know how many hours have passed
but i don't worry about it

i want to get back to those pages now
instead,
i let my heart drench
in this slow sunny noon

i hear the construction work outside
the drill,
the hammer,
breaking the silence
rhythmically,
i see a few random auto rickshaws,
and some cars and bikes,
visiting the quiet streets
in my neighborhood

there's no hustle-bustle,
no one's in a rush
as if everyone is trying to escape
from the monotony of the routine
on this weekend

it feels almost poetic
to find everything around so quiet
in a bustling city like mine

now i am already excited about
that fresh aroma of coffee
on the onset of sundown
that you're going to brew for us
in just a few minutes

and it's hard to get back to the book
so i just squeeze myself
in that tiny space next to you
and you pull me closer
even in your sleep
and i smile like a little girl
as i melt in your warm embrace
just like the sun is starting
to melt in the wide radiant sky
this evening…

Meet Me At The Sunset

meet me
at the horizon
when sky
flushes crimson

and
as we gaze at
yet another
serene sunset,

let me rest
on your shoulder
as you whisper
a sweet lullaby
in my ear

Reflection

the beauty
you find in me
is the
reflection
of your smile

the love
i find in you
is the
reflection
of my sorrow

What Is Love?

he often used to ask me,
'what is love?'

no matter what I say
it wasn't enough
for him to agree,

but today when
i looked at the moon,
it made my lips smile timidly
and my eyes dribbled
as my eyelids met,

it was he who came
to my mind
and i finally found
my answer
to his question

Raindrops

we meet
like lightning,

we kiss
like thunder,

we fall for each other
like raindrops,

and
the aroma of our love
lingers on in the air
like petrichor

Under The Same Moon

tonight,
i wish to share
a piece of my sky
with you

i wish to pour
all my happy stars
into your lap

and
i wish for us
to dream
under the same moon,

until the night
guards our
entangled hearts

I Found The Missing Piece Of My Soul

the moment
our eyes met
i felt tranquil

in your eyes,
i found
the missing piece
of my soul

and
my heartbeats
started singing
the hymns of
completeness

Just Breathe…

breathe like this is the last
we are going to be there for each other

breathe like there's no one else in this world
but just 'you' and 'me'

no,
don't utter a word,
just breathe...
like i'm the only aroma you need to inhale,
like i'm the only dream you love to chase,
like i'm the only future you wish to create,

just breathe...

breathe like a rhythm and make me sway,
breathe like a story and take me away,
breath like a hymn and let me pray,

no,
don't make any promises,
just breathe...
like you are the wind to my fire,
like you are the waves to my shore,
like you are the symphony to my despair,

just breathe...

breathe like the moon to my darkness,
breathe like the resplendent sky to my sunsets,
breathe like the dawn to my hopefulness,

no,
don't get lost in thoughts,
just breathe...
like a romantic movie,
no,
not the one with the pretty faces
and two lost souls in love
but breathe more like 'us',
where we are being our true selves

just breathe...

breathe like this is the last
we are going to be there for each other

breathe like there's no one else in this world
but just 'you' and 'me'

With You, I Live

we breathe,
we pray,
we feel,
we learn,
we dream,

but what
we forget
that we
are here
to live
not just
to exist

with you,
i live

i live
to the fullest,
blissfully,
soulfully
and
boundlessly

Resurrection

darling,
come sit next to me,
let me soothe
your tired soul
speak out your
darkest demons to me
not with your lips
but with your eyes
because
we could use our lips
for something
even better

oh dear,
trust me
with your heart,
hold my hands,
and plant a gentle kiss
on my palms,
help me
feel you tranquil
amidst all your
jittery thoughts

come closer honey,
and close your

weary eyes slowly,
let me embrace
all your scars
as you pull me closer
and stir up trembles
not just in my body
but also in my heart

sweet baby,
as you fill your lungs
with the *oriental florals*
on my neck,
my heart submits
to the *aromatic fougère*
aura of yours
and as we make love
to the melodic rhythm
of our favorite love songs,
we drown avidly in this
forbidden ocean of
love, lust and life

no sweetheart,
don't stop now,
make my eyes blush
by touching
all the uncharted places
within me,
not with your fingers

but with your lips
and i will open myself wide open
to welcome you home
as we gasp in ecstasy

my love,
let us sing the
breathless symphony of
pain and pleasure,
let us adorn each other
with the jewels
of our passionate desire
and
i promise
i will be your first kiss
even before dawn meets the skies
and
i will be your last desire
even before dreams meet your eyes

...And I Wait

i wake up
to see
the sunrise
in your eyes,
bright & fiery

i long
for the nights
to meet
the galaxy
in your arms,
mystical & infinite

and
the time
in between
i wait
for you
to come back

Your Moonlight

i might not
be your sun,
to shine
the light
on you

but
i will
always be
your moon,
to brighten up
your darkest
hours

It Was Always You

it was always
your soul
i worshiped,

it was always
your vibe
i discerned,

it was always
your heart
i adored,

it was always
your eyes
i found
myself into,

it was always
your body
i undressed under,

without you
i am just
bones and flesh
caged in misery

When I Go Back Home
Tonight

when i go back home tonight,
you won't be there,
and this idea itself is refraining me
from going back
to that empty space,
because my idea of home
is not those walls, doors and windows
but 'you'

when i go back home tonight,
i will ring the doorbell as usual
and a minute later,
i will bite my tongue,
as i remember
that you aren't around
and with a heavy heart,
i will open the door with the keys
hoping you'd appear magically from somewhere
with your goofy smile and a warm hug

when i go back home tonight,
our home will be
as uncluttered as i left it in the morning,
pillows would be puffed up,

bedsheet would be unwrinkled,
every corner of every room
would be spick and span,
just how i love it
but i would still fail to admire it
because whom would i scold
and pick silly fights with
for all the mess you make?

when i go back home tonight
i could watch
any of my favorite series peacefully,
i could finish
all the chores early,
and i could also
find some time to read
that incomplete novel uninterruptedly,

but instead,
i would just wear
your old, soft and fluffy t-shirt,
reminisce about our fond memories,
cuddle with your pillow,
and fill my lungs with your musky scent,
as i close my eyes

and as my tired mind and body
melt into my dreams

i would hope
for you to come back to me soon

31

Idea Of You

a part of me
still hopes
for you
to come back

and
a part of me
hates myself
for even
knowing you

and
then remains
the part
that is
bruised,
exhausted
and
disheartened
with this
whole idea of '*you*'

Shadows Of Your Memories

every sunset
brings back
memories of
me being me
by being yours

and
i sit still
until
my sorrows
get consumed
entirely
by the
bigger and darker
shadows of
those memories

I Hate You

every time when i say
i hate you,
it's a reminder to myself
that you aren't mine to love,
you never will,
and you never were

in fact,
you are not the love i need…

still there's this ache in my heart
when i say, i hate you
still there's sorrow in my eyes
when i think of you
still there's this urge
to hold you in my arms
when i see you

and
every time
i need to remind myself
of this invisible line
between being friends & being lovers

like
i could share love songs with you

but i need to remind myself
not to think of you
whenever i close my eyes
while humming those songs

like
i could share all my silly life problems
and little joys with you
but i need to remind myself
not to trouble you with my dilemma
when it comes to 'love'

like
i could only wish the best things for you
but i need to remind myself
not to imagine how our lives
would have been if we were together

and
that invisible line gets
more and more real
when i think of the times
when you still had a chance
to make a choice
and
i wasn't your first choice
or your last goodbye,
even then

i just hope,
someday,
this truth
would make me
so resentful and furious that
every time when i say
i hate you,
you would feel
my pain,
my anger
and my dejection

but maybe,
i am so engulfed
in this idea of love that
every time when i say
i hate you,
it's nothing but
just a gentle reminder to myself
that you aren't mine to love,
you never will,
and you never were

Missing You

missing you
is a story,
that begins
with me

and
invariably
ends at you

Fire & Ice

once again we meet
not like old lovers
or best of friends
but this time,

we meet more like
fire & ice

it's not our ephemeral
story of emotions
anymore,
but it's our
sweet blasphemy of
dark desires

i am the ice
blunt & frigid
and
you are the fire
untamed & torrid

there is a tsunami
between my legs
as we collide
and
we gasp for breath

as we unleash
the stormy demons
of our passion

our bodies dance
to the rhythm
of pain & pleasure
and
our moans melt into
each other's
poetic annihilation

no,
we don't want
to get lost
into each other
but
all we really want
is to be found
in this very moment
of wanting more

once again we meet
not like old lovers
or best of friends
but this time,

we meet more like
fire & ice

Our Love Story

on such nights,
desolate, cold and gloomy,
the moon accompanies
my melancholy

he fondly tells me
about the sun
and
i tell him
about our love story

The Failure

she fails
to understand
things he says

and
he fails
to say things
she understands

she wonders
if they fail
in love
miserably

or
love just
fails them
tragically
over & over
again

Love Is Unfair

my words
never did justice
to my feelings,
when i was
deeply in love with you

just like
my feelings
never did justice
to my words,
when you failed me
to believe in love
all over again

Poems About Love

on nights
like these
endless,
grim and dark,

i wrap a blanket
of words
around my
wretched heart
woven out
of poems
once i wrote
about love

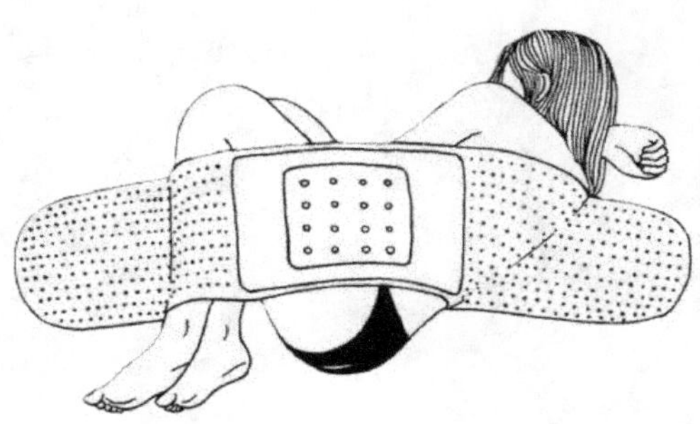

The End Is The Beginning

if dream is
the only place
where we can be 'us'

then i wish
to shut my eyes
once and for always…

www.ingramcontent.com/pod-product-compliance
Lightning Source LLC
Chambersburg PA
CBHW061725130726

47996CB00006B/2508